When Machines Understand Us

Understand Us

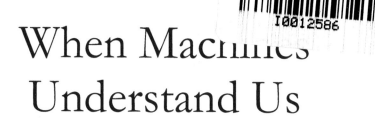

The Human Side of Emotional AI

Taylor Royce

DEDICATION

To everyone who works to create a more compassionate, interconnected world where technology improves people's lives and promotes understanding. In addition to the innumerable people whose voices will steer the ethical course for the future development of emotional technologies, this book is devoted to the innovators, intellectuals, and dreamers who believe in the potential of responsible AI. May this work serve as inspiration for a future in which compassion and creativity coexist and where, despite technological growth, we never lose sight of the human condition.

This is for you, the innovators and the change agents who help to create a society in which technology and people coexist with dignity and consideration.

DISCLAIMER

This book's content is provided solely for informational reasons. Although every attempt has been taken to guarantee the quality and dependability of the information presented here, neither the author nor the publisher offer any guarantees or claims about the content's completeness, accuracy, or applicability. The author's opinions are their own and may not represent those of any institutions or organizations with which they are associated.

Professional guidance in the areas of technology, law, ethics, or any other particular topic is not what this book is meant to offer. Before making decisions based on the information presented, readers are urged to speak with pertinent authorities or specialists.

Any actions or repercussions arising from the usage of the content in this book are not the responsibility of the author or publisher. The ethical, social, and legal ramifications of emotional AI and related technologies are complicated, and the subject is developing quickly. Readers should therefore be advised that as new research, best practices, and legislation are developed, the content in this book may change.

By reading this book, you understand and accept that neither the publisher nor the author will be held responsible for any hurt, loss, or damage brought on by using its contents.

CONTENTS

ACKNOWLEDGMENTS

I want to express my sincere gratitude to everyone who helped me along the way as I wrote this book. This project would not have been achieved without your support, wisdom, and unshakable faith in its worth.

I want to start by expressing my gratitude to my family and friends for their unwavering support, tolerance, and understanding. Your encouragement has been a rock, and I sincerely appreciate your faith in me through the good times and the bad on this journey.

This book's content has been inspired and shaped by the work of professionals, scholars, and thought leaders, for which I am also incredibly grateful. Your extensive and profound contributions to the domains of ethics, emotional intelligence, and artificial intelligence have greatly enhanced my comprehension of these intricate and quickly changing subjects.

I would especially like to thank my classmates, mentors, and coworkers for their insightful comments and helpful criticism, which have significantly enhanced this effort. Your viewpoints have improved the accuracy of this book and increased reader interest.

Finally, I want to thank all of the readers who have expressed interest in learning more about emotional AI and its ramifications. I'm motivated to keep exchanging thoughts and expertise by your enthusiasm and dedication to learning about this profession.

We appreciate everyone's input, advice, and steadfast support during this process. You own this book just as much as I do.

CHAPTER 1

EMOTIONAL AI FOUNDATIONS

1.1 Outlining Affective Computing and Emotional AI

Affective Computing, another name for emotional AI, is a subfield of artificial intelligence that focuses on identifying, analyzing, and reacting to human emotions. Emotional AI helps close the human-machine emotional gap by allowing technology to recognize and react to emotional cues in a contextually relevant way, whereas traditional AI systems are superior in logic, prediction, and data-driven learning.

The goal of emotional AI is to create systems that can recognize affective states in people and respond appropriately, not only robots that "feel." Emotional AI makes it possible for humans and machines to engage in ways that are more intuitive and empathetic, whether in social robotics, healthcare, education, or customer service.

Differentiating Between General and Emotional AI

The difference between general AI and emotional AI must be understood:

- The goal of general AI is to replicate human cognitive functions including learning, reasoning, problem-solving, and decision-making.
- The goal of Emotional AI, on the other hand, is to evaluate emotional states by analyzing non-verbal cues, facial expressions, tone of voice, and even physiological signals.

Although intelligent data processing is a component of both types of AI, emotional AI is uniquely human-centere in its goals and uses.

The Confluence of Artificial Intelligence, Neuroscience, and Psychology

By its very nature, emotional AI is multidisciplinary. It is located where three essential domains converge:

- The field of psychology offers fundamental frameworks for comprehending human emotions, including their causes and expressions.
- Neuroscience: Provides information about how the human brain processes emotions, which helps AI model or replicate these neural networks.
- The computational tools and methods required to process, learn from, and respond to emotional input are provided by Artificial Intelligence.

In emotionally charged settings like crisis counseling or elder care, this synergy enables robots to not only recognize emotions but also react in a socially and ethically responsible manner.

1.2 Historical Development and Significant Events

Both incremental increases in computer capabilities and shifting cultural expectations for human-technology interaction have contributed to the slow emergence of emotional artificial intelligence.

From Sentiment Analysis at an Early Stage to Advanced Affective Systems

Early sentiment analysis tools that tried to categorize text as neutral, negative, or positive based on keywords are where emotional artificial intelligence got its start. These systems lacked contextual sensitivity and were based on static rule sets.

However, the following brought about a change in the landscape:

- Real-time analysis of audio-visual data to identify changes in facial micro-expressions and tone; Neural networks that can model complex emotional nuances; Machine learning algorithms that learnt from massive emotion-tagged datasets

- The integration of multimodal data sources into contemporary emotional AI systems enables extremely precise emotion recognition across text, speech, video, and biometrics.

Important Trailblazers and Historic Research Advancements

In her 1997 book Affective Computing, Rosalind Picard of the MIT Media Lab formally introduced the field of Affective Computing. Picard presented the conceptual framework for machines that might connect with people in an empathic manner and maintained that emotional intelligence was necessary for really intelligent systems.

Important contributions consist of:

- The basis for facial emotion recognition systems was established by Paul Ekman's research on universal emotions and facial expressions.
- Multidimensional emotion modeling was influenced by Plutchik's emotion wheel.
- The creation of emotion-enabled robots that can communicate emotionally with people, such as Kismet (MIT).
- Affect-aware system development was influenced by cognitive science and neuroscience research.

These turning points laid the groundwork for today's emotional AI applications, which range from driver stress monitoring in autonomous cars to healthcare diagnostics.

1.3 The Study of Machine Emotions

A scientifically grounded framework that classifies, measures, and forecasts human emotional reactions is necessary for machines to "understand" emotions.

Emotion Models: Plutchik's Wheel and Ekman's Basic Emotions

The evolution of emotional AI has been greatly impacted by two main models:

- Six universal feelings are identified by Ekman's Six Basic feelings: happiness, sadness, fear, rage, surprise, and disgust
- Research from a variety of cultural backgrounds indicates that facial expressions are consistent.
- Widely utilized in surveillance AI and facial recognition systems

Plutchik's Wheel of Emotions:

- Presents the eight primary emotions: joy, trust, fear, surprise, sadness, disgust, anger, and anticipation.
- Shows how emotions interact and are intense.
- Assists machines in comprehending compound emotions and emotional gradients as they are arranged in a wheel.

These models enable emotional AI systems to incorporate the nuances and complexities of genuine human affect, going beyond binary emotion detection.

How Human Affect is Interpreted and Mimicked by Machines

To interpret emotional states, machines use a variety of modalities:

- Facial Expression Analysis: Linking emotional states to muscle movements through computer vision.
- Pitch, loudness, and tempo are evaluated for emotional clues in voice tone analysis.

- The use of natural language processing (NLP) to extract emotional sentiment from linguistic patterns is known as "text sentiment analysis."
- Biometric Feedback: Deciphering physiological markers including pupil dilation, heart rate, and galvanic skin response.

Once emotion has been identified, robots can imitate suitable reactions by:

- Virtual assistants with emotion-simulating avatars; voice answers with adaptive tone; and dynamic interfaces that adjust to the user's emotions (such as a soothing screen for a worried user)

- Although mimicry is not the same as empathy, it increases user pleasure and the illusion of social intelligence, particularly in high-stress situations like customer service or therapy bots.

1.4 Emotional AI's Core Technologies

Instead than being driven by a single invention, emotional

AI is a collection of interconnected technologies that combine to decode and respond to human emotion.

Processing Natural Language (NLP)

NLP makes it possible for machines to comprehend and evaluate human language. It is especially helpful in the context of emotional AI for:

- Identifying emotional keywords and tone from dialogue
- Contextual understanding of sarcasm, ambiguity, and emotional subtext
- Detecting sentiment from emails, social media, or chatbot interactions

The accuracy of emotion detection in text-based communication has significantly improved thanks to sophisticated NLP models like BERT, GPT, and RoBERTa.

Vision in Computers

Emotional cues are extracted from visual data by computer

vision systems. Among the applications are:

- Gaze tracking: Monitoring facial muscle movements to determine mood or response Posture recognition: Examining gestures and body language Recognizing user concentration, involvement, or anxiety

- Applications in automotive safety, telemedicine, and educational feedback systems rely heavily on these tools.

Biosensors

In order to deliver more profound emotional insights, biosensors gather physiological data. Among the examples are:

- Eg and ECG sensors: Skin conductance: Indicates emotional arousal; heart rate variability: Frequently used to gauge stress or relaxation Give cardiac and brain markers of mood.
- These products are particularly helpful for high-performance athlete training, mental health

monitoring, and wearable technology.

Systems for Multimodal Emotion Recognition

In order to create multimodal recognition frameworks, the most accurate emotional AI systems combine data from multiple channels simultaneously. These systems come together:

- Text (NLP)
- Audio (pitch and tone of voice)
- Visual (gestures and facial expressions)
- Biological cues (skin reaction, heart rate)

Multimodal systems obtain a more accurate and holistic picture of emotional state by combining these inputs, particularly in cases where emotional signals are confused or unclear.

Emotional AI is based on interdisciplinary collaboration, technological innovation, and rigorous science. The ability of AI to comprehend and react to human affect becomes not just a technical but also an ethical and psychological problem as it develops beyond logical reasoning systems into emotionally aware agents. people can investigate how Emotional AI is used in practical settings to change the way people live, work, and interact with technology by having a solid understanding of these fundamental concepts.

CHAPTER 2

EMOTIONAL AI's UNDERSTANDING OF US

2.1 Recognition of Facial Expressions

One of the most obvious ways that people convey their feelings is through their facial expressions. Indeed, facial expressions are globally recognized and frequently unintentional, which makes them perfect candidates for AI systems to detect emotions. Advanced algorithms that examine microexpressions and facial muscle movements are the foundation of emotional AI's capacity to decode facial expressions. These algorithms identify minute alterations in facial structure that correspond to particular emotions using computer vision and machine learning.

Algorithms Examining Facial Muscle Movements and Microexpressions

Algorithms that concentrate on identifying tiny,

involuntary facial movements, or microexpressions, are at the heart of facial expression identification. Though they usually only last a few seconds, these expressions convey a lot of emotional information. Among the main face muscles used are:

Corrugator supercilia (frowning) Frontalis (raised eyebrows) Zygomatic major (smiling)

AI can train to recognize these small muscle movements with increasing accuracy by using machine learning models, which are frequently based on massive datasets of facial photos labeled with emotional states. In this discipline, algorithms such as Convolutional Neural Networks (CNNs) are widely employed to categorize emotional states based on facial signals.

Cultural Interpretation Difficulties

Even with their effectiveness, facial expression recognition systems still have a lot of problems. One of the biggest obstacles is the cultural variation in how people communicate their emotions. For instance, even though a grin is typically connected to happiness, its meaning might change depending on the context in which it happens. Even when there isn't any enjoyment, smiling might be considered courteous in some cultures.

Furthermore, it might be challenging to attain 100% accuracy in cross-cultural applications because emotions like grief and anger can occasionally be portrayed identically across cultural boundaries. Therefore, it's imperative to modify facial recognition algorithms to take into consideration local cultural norms and variations in emotional expression. The resilience of these systems can be increased with further emotion theory and cross-cultural psychology study.

2.2 Emotion Analysis of Speech and Voice

Human communication is more than simply words; the speaker's tone, pitch, and rhythm all include a multitude of emotional information. In evaluating these vocal characteristics to identify emotional states, emotional AI has advanced significantly.

Identifying Emotions through Tone, Pitch, and Rhythm

To determine the underlying emotional state, voice emotion detection algorithms examine a variety of speech elements. Among the key features examined are:

- Pitch: While lower-pitched vocals may convey grief or rage, high-pitched tones may convey exhilaration or terror.
- Rhythm: Variations in speech rate, such as speaking more quickly, more slowly, or erratically, can indicate anxiety, excitement, or annoyance.
- Volume: A stronger voice tends to convey eagerness or wrath, whilst a softer voice may convey hesitancy or grief.

Voice emotion recognition systems use a combination of signal processing, machine learning, and natural language processing (NLP) to accurately infer emotions from speech, which is a dynamic and multifaceted signal. A neural network-based approach, for instance, might classify emotions like joyful, sad, furious, or nervous by examining how these features interact over time.

Uses in Call Centers and Virtual Assistants

Voice emotion analysis has been widely used in customer service contact centers and virtual assistants (Alexa, Siri, etc.). By examining variations in tone and cadence, virtual assistants may already identify user frustration. They can then modify their answers to be more sympathetic or provide more assistance. A system at a call center can prioritize a call or escalate it to a human agent if it detects emotional distress in the customer's voice.

AI-powered call center systems, for instance, may recognize a angry tone and react by referring the user to a representative who is capable of handling challenging talks or by providing calming statements. Making interactions with robots more human-like, intuitive, and emotionally aware is the aim of these applications.

2.3 Emotion Recognition Using Text

Another rich source of emotional information is text-based communication, such as emails, chat messages, and social media posts, in addition to voice cues and face expressions. While emotion classification goes a step further by identifying particular emotions like joy, rage, or sadness, sentiment analysis has long been used to determine whether a text's tone is positive, negative, or neutral.

Emotion Classification vs. Sentiment Analysis

Generally speaking, sentiment analysis divides texts into broad groups like neutral, negative, and positive. This method works well for figuring out a piece of writing's general tone, but it lacks the subtlety required to pinpoint certain emotional states.

On the other hand, Emotion classification seeks to distinguish between various emotions that are conveyed in text. While "I am overjoyed to hear the news!" would be categorized as expressing happiness, "I am so frustrated with this!" would be labeled as showing anger.

AI systems use Natural Language Processing (NLP) methods like text tokenization and word embedding to reliably identify emotions in text. AI is able to identify emotional undertones that more basic sentiment analysis technologies might overlook by examining the meaning of words and the context in which they occur.

Recognizing Delicate Emotional Signals in Electronic Communications

The absence of non-verbal cues in written words, such as voice tone or facial expressions, which are crucial for contextualizing human emotions, is one of the difficulties with text-based emotion identification. AI models now include contextual analysis, syntax analysis, and word choice evaluation in order to get around this restriction.

For example, depending on the larger context, a seemingly neutral statement like "I'm fine" could convey annoyance or sarcasm. In a similar vein, emojis have emerged as an essential component of internet communication, giving text a deeper emotional dimension. It is now necessary to train AI to understand the meaning of emojis and how they affect the feeling of the whole.

Furthermore, as AI must precisely identify emotions in a variety of linguistic and cultural contexts, multilingual capabilities are becoming more and more crucial in this field. Large, varied datasets are needed for training, and models must be carefully adjusted to account for particular language quirks.

2.4 Monitoring of Physiological Signals

Physiological cues are one of the most accurate ways to comprehend human emotions. In applications like healthcare, mental health monitoring, and security where emotional awareness is essential, these signals such as heart rate, skin conductance, and brainwave activity offer real-time insights into an individual's emotional state.

EEG, Emotion Inference, Heart Rate, and Galvanic Skin Response

- Heart Rate (HR): An individual's heart rate frequently rises when they are feeling anxious or excited. Heart rate variations can be tracked by AI systems to determine whether a person is stressed or anxious.
- The Galvanic Skin Response, or GSR, is a

measurement of the skin's electrical conductance, which rises in response to emotional arousal. This is frequently employed in consumer research to evaluate emotional engagement or to uncover lies.

- Electroencephalogram (EEG): EEG tracks brainwave activity, and certain patterns like calmness, alertness, or mental fatigue are linked to particular emotions.

A comprehensive emotional profile is produced by combining physiological signals with other data points, such as voice tone, facial expressions, and text sentiment. The accuracy and dependability of emotion detection are improved by this multi-signal method.

The Moral Consequences of Biometric Monitoring

Although there are many advantages to using biometric data for emotion detection, especially in mental health and customer service, there are also serious ethical concerns. Individual privacy may be violated by the collecting of sensitive information like heart rate or skin response. There is also the possibility of misuse, in which emotional information may be used for behavioral control, surveillance, or manipulative marketing.

- People must be fully informed about the types of data being collected and how they will be used in order to obtain their consent.
- Bias: Emotional AI, like other AI systems, may inherit biases from its training data, which could result in unfair or erroneous emotional judgments, especially for specific groups.
- Data Security: To avoid unwanted access or exploitation, emotionally sensitive information must be managed and stored securely.

Establishing clear standards and regulations will be essential as emotional AI develops further to guarantee that its use respects privacy and protects against abuse.

The advanced techniques used by Emotional AI systems to comprehend and interpret human emotions have been discussed in this chapter. Every technique, including voice analysis, text-based detection, facial expression recognition, and physiological signal monitoring, offers important information about the user's emotional state. But each has its own set of difficulties, such as ethical concerns, contextual subtleties, or cultural differences. While comprehending these techniques and their uses opens the door to more human-like and sympathetic AI systems, it also encourages greater in-depth consideration of our responsibilities in creating emotionally intelligent technology.

CHAPTER 3

HUMAN-CENTERED DESIGN IN AFFECTIVE SYSTEMS

3.1 Creating Interfaces with Empathy

The creation of emotion-aware systems that react to human emotions in a manner that resembles empathy is the foundation of affective computing. The user experience may be significantly improved by designing interfaces that are both emotionally intelligent and functional, making interactions more personalized and meaningful. In order to create a sense of trust and connection, human-centered design aims to make sure that the system's emotional reactions are aligned with the user's needs.

Developing Emotionally Intelligent Response Systems

Systems that comprehend, analyze, and react to human emotions in real-time must be designed in order to produce empathic interfaces. This necessitates incorporating emotion recognition algorithms into the functionality of the interface. When a user feels frustrated with an application, for example, a well-designed emotion-aware system would recognize this from their voice tone, facial expressions, or even their body language and respond accordingly, possibly by offering support or encouraging remarks.

In order to make the interaction feel more natural and human-like, the most sophisticated systems are those that can modify their responses in response to emotional cues. Among these systems' salient characteristics are:

- Real-time emotion detection: This method uses biosensors, computer vision, or speech analysis to identify user emotions in real time.
- Dynamic emotional responses: Modifying the language, tone, and support systems of the system in reaction to emotional information.
- Responding to emotions within the broader context of the conversation rather than in isolation is known as "context awareness."

These systems are meant to mimic emotional

intelligence, which is more than just identifying feelings; it also includes adjusting to the user's emotional state and responding appropriately. To improve the user experience and increase motivational support, a virtual tutor could, for example, recognize a student's frustration and change the lesson's difficulty level.

Applications in Customer Service, Therapy, and Education

In industries where recognizing and reacting to emotions is essential, such education, therapy, and customer service, the use of emotion-aware interfaces has shown impressive results.

- Education: To enhance student engagement and modify classes to meet emotional requirements, learning platforms can incorporate emotion-aware systems. An AI-powered tutoring system, for example, may recognize when a student is having trouble understanding a concept and offer more clarifications, examples, or even inspirational ideas. These kinds of systems help create individualized learning experiences that promote success and engagement over the long run.

- Therapy: Emotion recognition-enabled virtual therapy assistants can identify small emotional changes in a patient's voice or facial expression throughout a session. Reassurance, modifying therapy approaches, or indicating when a more in-depth discussion is required can all be accomplished with the use of this data. Therapists can gain important insights into their patients' emotional health by using these AI-powered assistants to monitor emotional development over time.

- Customer Support: Chatbots with emotional intelligence are able to interpret a customer's tone and sentiment and modify their responses accordingly. A chatbot may, for instance, hear annoyance in a customer's speech and react more sympathetically and perceptively, defusing possible confrontations and enhancing the client experience in general.

3.2 Context-Awareness and Personalization

User engagement and happiness can be greatly increased by affective systems that personalize their answers according to the emotional context. In order to provide a feeling of individualized attention, emotional AI can make decisions based on a user's past interactions, preferences, and the current context of the encounter. User history and context-awareness are two essential elements of personalization in emotion-aware design.

Tailoring Emotional Reactions according to Context and User History

The ability to adjust emotional reactions based on past interactions and known user preferences is one of the core components of customization. AI systems can forecast the emotional tone that would work best in a particular circumstance by examining a user's prior actions, feelings, and reactions. For example:

- An emotional customer service representative In

order to prevent reoccurring unpleasant encounters, AI may recall a user's prior annoyances and provide a more calming tone or proactive solutions.

- When a fitness app recognizes stress or fatigue in the user's voice or biometric data, it could provide more encouragement during exercises, while reducing it when the user is confident or excited.

Context-awareness is also very important. Situationally appropriate emotional reactions are required. A system should, for instance, be able to recognize when a user is in a high-stress situation and offer more calming and helpful input. Conversely, a user may respond more positively and enthusiastically if they are in a celebratory mood. The system feels more human-like and responsive to the fluctuating nature of emotional states as a result of this flexibility.

Hazards of Emotional Misinterpretation and Overfitting

Over-reliance on customisation, however, carries some hazards. The possibility of overfitting is a major obstacle.

An emotional AI system may overlook new emotional cues or react incorrectly to shifts in the user's emotional state if it bases its reactions too heavily on past exchanges. For instance, the system may over-correct, providing excessive comfort when a more neutral response would be more suitable, if the user's usual attitude is one of dissatisfaction.

Another risk is emotional misinterpretation. An AI system may give answers that seem intrusive or overly familiar if it misunderstands or overinterprets minor emotional cues, which could undermine user confidence. For instance, an overzealous greeting during a time of personal sorrow may cause discomfort or alienation. To prevent such issues, thorough system design and ongoing performance monitoring are necessary to strike the correct balance in emotional personalization.

3.3 Trust and User Experience

Any human-centered design approach must be based on trust, particularly when it comes to emotion-aware technologies. Users' trust and contentment will be jeopardized if they believe a system is too manipulative or, on the other hand, lacks emotional intelligence. As a result, developing emotionally intelligent systems that not only comprehend emotions but also behave in genuine and respectful ways is crucial.

Improving Credibility and Interaction Satisfaction With Emotion-Aware Design

Enhancing user experience (UX) through a smooth and sympathetic engagement should always be the main goal when creating emotion-aware technology. The following are some essential design guidelines to improve UX in emotion-aware systems:

- Making sure that emotional reactions fit the interaction's general tone and context is known as consistency.
- In order to build trust and prevent hidden motives, users should be able to tell when an AI system is reacting to emotional cues.
- Subtlety: Feelings shouldn't be overpowering or invasive. The AI ought to be able to strike a balance between demonstrating empathy and honoring the

user's independence.

When these concepts are successfully incorporated into an emotion-aware interface, the system's credibility will rise and interaction satisfaction will be improved. Higher retention rates, improved user engagement, and improved system perceptions result from this.

Juggling Complexity and Transparency

Transparency is essential, but it's also critical to avoid overwhelming the user with excessive complexity. If users are continuously reminded of the system's emotional analysis, they may grow suspicious or uneasy. For example, a health monitoring system may employ emotional data to measure a person's well-being. The difficulty is in maintaining appropriate transparency, which allows users to have faith in the system's abilities without being overloaded with details or complexity.

Additionally, by making the interaction more fluid and less robotic, simplifying emotional responses can improve the user experience. Systems should respond in ways that are situationally aware and nuanced, aiming for emotional nuances rather than overt gestures.

3.4 Emotion AI's Inclusivity and Accessibility

Emotional AI must be inclusive and accessible as it gets increasingly ingrained in our daily lives. This involves acknowledging the variety of emotional expression and experience, including variations among culturally diverse and neurodiverse communities.

Identifying Culturally and Neurodiverse Emotional Expressions

Different users have different ways of expressing their feelings. Emotional AI systems need to take into consideration the fact that neurodiverse individuals, like those with autism spectrum disorder (ASD), may have trouble identifying or expressing emotions in conventional ways. A person with ASD, for instance, might display emotional states that are different from the standard facial expressions or speech modulations that the majority of AI systems are trained to identify.

Designing emotional AI also poses special obstacles for culturally varied communities. Emotions can be conveyed differently in different cultures, as was covered in previous sections. For example, East Asian cultures may show anger differently from Western cultures, therefore it is important for AI systems to understand and adjust to these cultural nuances.

Avoiding AI Bias and Marginalization

An additional urgent problem is the possibility of AI bias. Inaccurate emotional recognition may arise from the marginalization of particular groups if the data utilized to train emotional AI systems is not diverse enough. This may be avoided by using inclusive design techniques, which guarantee that training data originates from a wide range of cultural backgrounds, neurotypes, and emotional expression styles.

Furthermore, prejudice can be lessened and personalized inclusivity improved by developing user controls that let people modify how emotional AI systems perceive and react to their feelings. Users can now customize emotional exchanges thanks to this.

based on their personal preferences, making the system as a whole more respectful and empathetic.

Creating inclusive, individualized, and sympathetic affective systems is a challenging but worthwhile undertaking. We may design systems that improve user pleasure, cultivate deep connections, and honor the range of human emotional expression by emphasizing emotional intelligence, trust, and accessibility. Maintaining a balance between technological capabilities and human-centered design principles is crucial as emotion-aware technology develops to make sure that these systems meet the requirements of all users in a way that is inclusive, efficient, and respectful.

CHAPTER 4

PRACTICAL APPLICATIONS OF EMOTIONAL AI IN ACTION

4.1 Sentiment-Aware Chatbots and Customer Support

AI-powered chatbots have transformed customer service in recent years by increasing interaction speed and efficiency. Emotion-aware chatbots, which are able to recognize and react to users' emotional states, represent the next frontier in this field. Businesses are now able to offer more personalized and empathetic experiences with the use of affective computing into customer service chatbots. In order to determine a customer's emotional state, these systems examine both verbal and non-verbal clues, including tone, word choice, and typing speed.

Real-Time Identification of Satisfaction or Frustration

Real-time emotion detection and interpretation by sentiment-aware chatbots is what gives them their strength.

Chatbots can recognize emotions such as frustration, satisfaction, anger, or happiness from the customer's words by using natural language processing (NLP) and sentiment analysis. Because of this flexibility, chatbots can modify their responses to make consumers feel heard and understood.

For example, if a consumer uses terms like "angry," "disappointed," or "frustrated" to communicate frustration over a delayed shipment, the chatbot can identify negative sentiment and instantly change its tone by using apologetic language or proposing solutions that show empathy. This can turn a potentially bad experience into a good one and defuse potential conflict. On the other hand, the chatbot may react enthusiastically when a consumer shows satisfaction, reiterating a satisfying interaction and promoting more interaction in the future.

Adaptive Conversation Creation for Better Assistance

The ability to adaptive dialogue generation allows emotionally intelligent chatbots to modify their responses according to the emotional context of the exchange. These technologies adapt the dialogue dynamically rather than merely following a predetermined flow, guaranteeing that the user's emotional condition is suitably addressed.

For instance:

- When a customer is calm and just wants to know about a product, the chatbot can give informational responses that concentrate on specifics and features.
- The chatbot can change to a more empathetic tone when a consumer is upset or furious, providing solutions and apologies, and if needed, elevating the conversation to a human representative.

By allowing the chatbot to manage a greater spectrum of client emotions and circumstances, its ability to transition between various emotional tones and styles not only increases user satisfaction but also boosts the effectiveness of support systems.

4.2 Medical Treatment and Mental Health

Emotion-aware AI has also made great progress in the

healthcare sector, especially in the area of mental health. emotion AI presents promising solutions for both early detection and intervention, given the growing need for mental wellness support and the scarcity of mental health professionals in many areas.

AI for Early Anxiety and Depression Detection

In order to track patients' emotional states and offer early warnings concerning illnesses like depression and anxiety, emotion AI is being utilized in healthcare more and more. Artificial intelligence (AI) systems can identify indications of emotional distress before a person is even aware that they are having difficulties by examining speech patterns, facial expressions, and text input.

For instance, emotion AI may be used by a mental health app to examine a user's written or spoken communication over time. An alert may be triggered by abrupt changes in speech rate, tone, or word choice (e.g., statements of negativity or hopelessness). Proactive intervention, including suggesting resources, offering coping mechanisms, or even putting the user in touch with a mental health specialist, is made possible by this early detection system.

Healthcare professionals might potentially lessen the effect of mental health crises and improve patient outcomes by identifying these emotional markers and providing timely assistance.

Companion Bots for Emotional Monitoring and Elder Care

Emotion AI is being used in elderly care as well as clinical settings. For older people, especially those who might be lonely or have restricted access to social contacts, emotional intelligence-enabled companion robots offer both companionship and emotional monitoring. These systems deliver valuable insights to family members and caregivers by monitoring not just physical health but also mental and emotional well-being.

For example, by examining an old person's speech patterns, daily routines, or facial expressions, a companion robot may identify symptoms of loneliness or depression. To help patients feel less alone, the robot can then do things like reminding them to take their meds, providing emotional support, or even striking up a conversation. When a notable emotional or physical shift is noticed, these systems may also alert caregivers, allowing for timely intervention and care.

In times of crisis, as the COVID-19 epidemic, when many older individuals experienced increased emotional discomfort and loneliness, the function of emotion-aware technologies in elder care has been particularly beneficial.

4.3 Learning and Adaptive Education

Emotion-aware systems are revolutionizing learning in education by making it more responsive, engaging, and interactive. Teachers may now design individualized experiences that react to students' emotional states by incorporating emotional intelligence into learning platforms and tutoring systems. This improves learning outcomes and student happiness.

Systems for Emotion-Aware Tutoring

AI-driven tutoring programs with emotion detection capabilities can give individualized feedback according to the student's emotional state. An emotion-aware tutoring system, for instance, can identify a student's displeasure with a challenging math problem by analyzing their voice tone, facial expressions, or even their keystrokes. The system can then reply with adjusted teaching strategies or encouraging messages. The system may provide a more motivational tone to encourage the student to keep going or simpler questions to boost confidence.

Additionally helpful for adaptive learning, emotion-aware tutoring systems adjust the pace and level of difficulty of lessons according to the student's emotional engagement. The system can slow down and provide more assistance if a learner is having trouble and displaying symptoms of impatience. The system might present more difficult content to a student who is actively participating and showing excitement.

By establishing an environment that adjusts to the emotional and cognitive requirements of every learner, these emotionally intelligent systems assist in optimizing learning experiences.

Improving Learner Involvement and Identifying Cognitive Stress

Emotion AI is essential to comprehending cognitive overload and student engagement, two factors that are essential to successful learning. For example, the system can modify the lesson to re-engage the learner with more engaging or entertaining content if they are displaying symptoms of boredom or disengagement (such as yawning, lack of eye contact, or a slow response time).

On the other hand, the system can identify cognitive overload and modify the lesson to lessen the cognitive load if a student exhibits symptoms of stress or overwhelm (such as heavy sighs, frustration, or rapid speaking). This could be delivering encouragement, allowing relaxation periods, or simplifying the content. Emotion-aware educational systems maintain the effectiveness and enjoyment of the learning process by constantly adapting to the emotional and cognitive states of the students.

4.4 Promotion and Marketing

The use of emotion-aware AI in marketing and advertising signifies a significant change in the way that companies interact with their target audience. In order to increase the success of marketing campaigns, emotionally intelligent systems are making it possible for hyper-personalized advertising to directly appeal to consumers' emotional triggers. But this also brings up moral questions about using emotions to one's advantage.

Customized Content Delivery and Emotional Targeting

Marketers can now target customers based on their emotional state and transcend traditional demographics thanks to emotion AI. Artificial intelligence (AI) systems may provide emotionally tailored content to people at the appropriate moment by examining their speech, facial expressions, and even their online activity. This elicits the desired emotional response and increases engagement.

For instance:

- Ads for comfort wear may be displayed to a user on a fashion website if the system notices indications of weariness or stress.

- When someone exhibits signs of irritation or disappointment, an emotionally intelligent advertising system may display a motivational advertisement in an effort to improve their mood and encourage constructive interaction.

Higher conversion rates and increased sales can result from more effective marketing techniques that communicate directly to consumers' emotions through personalized emotional targeting.

Neuromarketing and Manipulation Ethics

Even though emotion-aware advertising works, there are serious ethical issues with it, especially when it comes to neuromarketing. Neuromarketing can result in extremely manipulative strategies by analyzing neurological and psychological reactions to advertising using emotion AI. Marketers might construct advertisements that take advantage of weaknesses or establish emotional dependence on items by knowing a consumer's emotional triggers. This would encourage people to make purchases they may not need or desire.

There is continuous discussion about the ethics of manipulation in emotional targeting. Some contend that personalization improves customer experiences and results in more relevant ads, but others caution that it can also be exploited to manipulate emotions, particularly among vulnerable groups. In order to ensure that these technologies improve the customer experience without going against ethical standards, marketers must be transparent, obtain consumer agreement, and employ emotion AI appropriately.

Emotion-aware AI has demonstrated tremendous promise in marketing, healthcare, education, and customer service, offering chances for more individualized interactions, improved results, and deeper engagement. However, to guarantee that the advantages of emotional AI are realized without jeopardizing individual rights, the power of these systems must be restrained by rigorous consideration of ethics, privacy, and user well-being. As this technology develops further, it will surely influence how people engage with machines and with one other, resulting in more emotionally aware and sympathetic systems in a variety of sectors.

CHAPTER 5

EMOTIONAL AI IN SOCIAL INTERACTION AND ROBOTICS

5.1 Social Robots with Emotional Awareness

A new generation of robots that can not only complete tasks but also interact with people in ways that demonstrate an awareness of emotional states has been made possible by the integration of emotional AI with robotics. Due to their ability to perceive and react to human emotions, these emotionally aware robots are a crucial part of industries such as healthcare, hospitality, retail, and caregiving. Robots' capacity to sense and respond to emotions has completely changed how people interact with machines, especially in contexts that call for social connection, empathy, and emotional sensitivity.

From Pepper to Sophia: "Feeling" Robots.

Pepper and Sophia are two of the most well-known

instances of emotionally intelligent robots, and they have both drawn international attention for their ability to recognize emotions in a manner similar to that of a human.

Pepper: SoftBank Robotics created Pepper, which can interpret emotions from body language and facial expressions. Pepper can provide customized responses by identifying and reacting to the emotional tone of a person's speech and facial expressions thanks to its emotion recognition software. Pepper's ability to interact has been used in customer service, where it interacts with clients by modifying its answers in reaction to their emotional cues. Pepper's emotional intelligence improves consumer experiences by offering a more intimate, sympathetic engagement, whether in the retail or hotel industries.

Hanson Robotics developed Sophia, a sophisticated humanoid robot that can participate in more intricate social interactions. Sophia can show emotions like happiness, sadness, and anger since her facial expressions are made to resemble those of people. It interprets human speech and produces suitable emotional reactions using natural language processing (NLP). Applications for Sophia may be found in many domains, including as media, education, and customer service, where its capacity to empathize with people has been a useful tool.

Even while the two robots take different tacks when it comes to emotional engagement, they both mark a substantial advancement in the creation of robots that are capable of meaningful social connection in addition to mechanical jobs.

Uses in Retail, Healthcare, and Hospitality

Numerous sectors have identified applications for emotionally intelligent robots:

- Retail: To improve consumer interaction, retail settings are utilizing robots like Pepper. Such robots can contribute to the creation of a more welcoming environment by identifying the emotions of its customers. In addition to responding to complaints with empathy and greeting customers with the proper emotional warmth, they can even help with sales by interpreting cues and suggesting goods that suit a customer's tastes or mood.

- Caregiving: Emotionally intelligent robots can keep an eye on the emotional health of the elderly, providing company and reducing feelings of isolation. Additionally, these robots could assist older people with memory and cognitive issues by reminding them to take their meds or appointments, or even by conversing with them to lessen their sense of loneliness.

- hotel: By providing individualized services, welcoming guests, and adjusting to their emotional requirements, emotionally intelligent robots can improve the hotel industry's guest experiences. Robots may, for instance, greet anxious business travelers with a smile or engage in calming conversation with visitors who want emotional support.

Robots that can identify and react to emotional cues provide more personalized and empathetic services in all of these domains, which eventually raises customer satisfaction and fosters constructive relationships.

5.2 Emotional Bonding Between Humans and Robots

Humans have started to develop emotional attachments to increasingly sophisticated and emotionally intelligent robots. The future of human-robot relationships and the psychological effects of these attachments are important issues raised by this phenomena, which is frequently referred to as human-robot emotional bonding.

Anthropomorphism and Emotional Attachment

Anthropomorphizing, or giving non-human things human characteristics, is a natural human tendency. This is particularly true when engaging with emotionally intelligent robots that can imitate human facial expressions and actions. People frequently treat robots as friends or even companions, demonstrating the importance of anthropomorphism in creating emotional bonds.

For example, elderly people may develop deep emotional bonds with social robots in caregiving environments. These robots can display behaviors that give the impression that they are sympathetic, such as comforting tones or facial expressions of worry, even though they are not actually able to feel emotions. The elderly may start to see the robot as a buddy, which might help their mental health, especially if they are lonely.

Children may develop relationships to learning-assistance robots in educational environments. The youngster can receive regular emotional response from these robots, which will help them feel acknowledged and appreciated. The child can start to see the robot as an emotional partner and supportive tutor.

Advantages and Effects on the Mind

Emotional attachment to robots has important benefits.

- Emotional support: Robots can offer emotional support and companionship, which helps lessen loneliness, particularly in older people or those who don't socialize often.
- Engagement and motivation: Emotionally responsive

robots can motivate people in therapeutic or educational contexts by providing calming interactions or positive reinforcement when the person is in distress.

- Therapeutic benefits: Robots can be a non-threatening companion for people who struggle with social or emotional issues, providing therapeutic treatments in a secure setting.

But there are psychological implications to take into account:

- Dependency: One worry is that people who develop emotional bonds with robots may become over-dependent, depending on them for emotional support instead of building human connections.
- People run the risk of misinterpreting the robot's emotional reactions as real, which could result in an emotional bond based on an artificial relationship. This is because robots are unable to actually feel emotions.
- Ethical considerations: The morality of building robots that evoke powerful emotions makes one

wonder if it is appropriate to build robots that have the ability to control human emotions, particularly in populations who are more susceptible.

Despite these reservations, further research is needed to fully understand the psychological effects of emotional bonding between humans and robots and how to best utilize these connections for positive societal outcomes.

5.3 Robotic Expressive Behaviors

Robots' expressive behaviors are one of the most potent ways they may emotionally connect with people. These acts make interactions more natural and human-like by enabling robots to express intentions and feelings without using words. Facial expressions, gestures, and voice modulation are examples of expressive behaviors that influence how people view and respond to robots.

Voice modulation, gestures, and facial expressions

It is possible to equip robots with screens or facial characteristics that mimic human facial expressions, such as frowning, smiling, or raising eyebrows. Interactions feel more natural when these phrases are used to communicate feelings and intentions. For instance, a robot made to assist kids with learning problems might give them a smile when they successfully answer a question or a concerned look when they seem perplexed or irritated.

- Gestures: Physical gestures like pointing and nodding can also be used by robots to communicate. By incorporating a layer of nonverbal interaction that mimics human behavior, these gestures can improve communication. Robots can provide emotional input beyond words by using gestures to reassure or comfort people in therapeutic situations.

- The emotional quality of an interaction can be greatly impacted by the tone, pitch, and speed of a robot's voice. While a more animated voice may express excitement or encouragement, a pleasant, soothing tone can assist calm people who are nervous. For robots to be able to react correctly to the emotional cues of the people they interact with, this component of emotional AI is essential.

Configuring Emotion Display for Perceptive Communication

It's difficult to program robots to exhibit emotionally suitable behaviors. The robot's motions and facial expressions must be contextually appropriate and in line with the user's emotional state, according to engineers. While a robot working with a child in a learning context might use enthusiastic gestures and a playful tone, a robot dealing with a worried client in a retail setting should employ calming gestures and a soothing voice.

The secret to producing smooth, emotionally impactful experiences is the intuitive nature of these interactions. Humans may interact with robots more readily when they exhibit expressive behaviors that are emotionally accurate. This lowers barriers between humans and machines and promotes stronger emotional bonds.

5.4 Robots in Education and Therapy

Robots with emotional intelligence are revolutionizing

therapy and education by providing new approaches to learning and treatment. These robots can offer tailored assistance to people with particular requirements, such as mental health support, autism, or trauma recovery, by utilizing emotional intelligence.

Social Robots for the Recovery from Autism and Trauma

Social robots are being utilized as tools to help youngsters with autism develop their emotional and social abilities. These robots can mimic social interactions, giving kids a safe space to practice identifying and reacting to emotions. In contrast to human interaction, robots provide a nonjudgmental presence that can be especially helpful for kids who struggle in social settings.

In a similar vein, robots can serve as emotional support systems for people recuperating from trauma. In a world that is unpredictable, their steady and predictable actions offer stability. Emotion AI-enabled robots, for instance, can assist patients in identifying and controlling their emotions by suggesting stress-reducing methods or just being a reassuring, reliable presence.

Setting an Emotional Example in Special Education Settings

Robots with emotional intelligence are being employed in special education settings to model emotional behavior for students who struggle with behavior or learning. These robots can give emotional feedback, model appropriate emotional expression, and even modify their answers in reaction to the conduct of the pupil. Students can benefit from this modeling in the areas of self-awareness, social interaction, and emotional regulation.

Teachers can provide more individualized and successful learning experiences by incorporating emotionally intelligent robots into special education, guaranteeing that kids' emotional requirements are met OR are satisfied while encouraging advancement in academic development and emotional development.

The crucial role that emotionally intelligent robots play in influencing human-robot relationships has been discussed in this chapter. From developing emotionally intelligent machines to encouraging emotional bonding and expressive behaviors, the area is making rapid progress in providing robots that are able to comprehend and react to human emotions in addition to performing tasks. These robots' educational and therapeutic uses are especially remarkable, with the potential to revolutionize sectors from autism to trauma recovery. As robots advances, the incorporation of emotional AI has the potential to fundamentally alter how humans engage with technology.

CHAPTER 6

EMOTIONAL MANIPULATION, BIAS, AND ETHICS

6.1 Emotion Misreading and Algorithmic Bias

The usage of artificial intelligence (AI) systems has raised increasing ethical questions as they continue to gain popularity, especially in the area of emotion recognition. The algorithmic bias that can skew emotional readings and result in misinterpretations of human emotions is one of the biggest problems with emotional AI. These biases are not only theoretical; they have practical repercussions, especially when emotion-detecting algorithms are used in delicate fields like law enforcement, healthcare, education, and hiring.

Cultural, racial, and gender biases in emotion recognition

It has been demonstrated that emotion identification

algorithms, which examine speech tones, facial expressions, and other physiological indicators, display biases according to cultural context, gender, and race. These biases result from a number of things, including the subjective nature of emotional expression itself, the assumptions included into the programming, and the data sets used to train the algorithms.

- Racial bias: A number of studies have shown that emotion detection systems are less able to identify emotions in people of various races, especially Black and Asian people, when they are trained on primarily Caucasian data sets. An algorithm that reads facial expressions, for instance, might misread a Black person's emotional state and perceive neutral expressions as hostile or angry.

- Gender bias: How emotions are interpreted is also influenced by gender preconceptions. It might be difficult for AI systems to identify emotions in a way that reflects gender norms. Men's emotions may be underrepresented or disregarded, frequently being read as indifferent or unfeeling. In contrast, women's emotions, especially in professional contexts, are more likely to be perceived as overly emotional or irrational.

- Cultural bias: various cultures have various ways of expressing emotions, and some behaviors that could be considered angry in one culture may be interpreted differently in another. For example, East Asian cultures tend to be more restrained when it comes to emotional actions, whereas Western cultures tend to show their emotions more directly. Significant cultural misreadings result when emotion AI is trained primarily on Western emotions, failing to take these variances into consideration.

In addition to being troublesome, these biases can have dangerous implications in fields like law enforcement (where emotion detection technology may misinterpret stress or anxiety, resulting in unfair profiling) and recruitment (where algorithms may inadvertently favor one demographic over another).

Unintended Consequences Case Studies

- Recruiting Algorithms: According to a 2018 study, recruiting platforms that use artificial intelligence (AI) to evaluate candidates' emotional intelligence significantly favor male candidates while misinterpreting female candidates' emotional expressions. Because the algorithms incorrectly penalized women for displaying emotions that are typically linked with lack of confidence in professional contexts, such as nervousness or uncertainty, this resulted in a gender imbalance in hiring procedures.

- Criminal Justice: In one contentious instance, a police force's emotion recognition system incorrectly recognized fear in suspects, frequently classifying anxious people as guilty or deceptive. For marginalized populations in particular, this could result in unjustified scrutiny or false allegations.

These illustrations highlight the need for developers to take these concerns into consideration while creating and deploying these technologies, as well as the far-reaching effects of algorithmic bias in emotional AI.

6.2 Privacy, Monitoring, and Consent

A significant concern that has surfaced with the increasing use of emotional AI is privacy and the gathering of emotion-related data. Serious questions about consent, surveillance, and the ethical boundaries of data gathering are brought up by AI systems' capacity to recognize and record emotional reactions.

Gathering Emotional Data and the Informed Consent Issue

Emotion recognition methods frequently need access to personal data, including physiological markers like heart rate, voice tone, and facial expressions. The emotional information collected by these systems can be quite sensitive and personal in contexts such as smartphones, consumer products, or online interactions. A consumer app might, for instance, monitor a user's emotional reactions to material or ads in order to compile a thorough emotional profile that might be utilized for product recommendations or targeted marketing.

- The main question is whether people have given their informed consent and are fully aware that their emotional data is being collected. Emotional data delves deeper into people's psychological state than standard data collecting, which concentrates on demographic data (like age or location). However, a lot of people might not be completely aware of how much of their emotional reactions are being monitored or the potential uses of this information.

- Informed consent is essential yet frequently lacking. Users frequently agree to use an app or service without understanding the full scope of emotion tracking. Furthermore, people find it challenging to completely comprehend the risks and implications of their consent due to the lack of transparency in the processing and storage of emotional data.

- An additional issue of concern is data ownership. Who is the owner of the user-generated emotional data? Is it the individual user, the app developers, or outside advertisers? These issues are still mostly unanswered and add to the growing worries about emotional privacy.

Emotional profiling and surveillance capitalism

Shoshana Zuboff came up with the phrase surveillance capitalism to characterize a new economic system in which personal data, particularly emotional data, is commodified and utilized to forecast and affect customer behavior. Businesses can make money by compiling highly individualized emotional profiles of people and using this data to create manipulative content or more convincing marketing campaigns.

- Emotional profiling: Based on how people respond to various stimuli, emotional AI systems generate in-depth psychological profiles. A website might, for example, monitor users' emotional reactions to various ad formats in order to optimize future adverts for maximum engagement.

- It is feared that these profiles may be utilized to

manipulate individuals on a subconscious level targeted manipulation. Businesses can develop experiences that encourage people to do things like buy a product, share personal information, or interact with content that may not be in their best interests by appealing to particular emotions, such as fear, excitement, or desire.

- Surveillance capitalism has significant ethical ramifications. Scalable emotional manipulation marks a significant change in how computers may shape and control human behavior, posing major privacy and autonomy issues.

6.3 Psychological Impact and Emotional Manipulation

Emotional manipulation is made possible by the development of emotionally intelligent systems, which also holds enormous promise for improving human-machine interactions. This section looks at the psychological effects of using emotional AI to influence, corrupt, or even take advantage of people.

Design Persuasion and Emotional Support

Persuasive design is one of the most used techniques for manipulating emotions in digital systems. This method focuses on exploiting psychological triggers and emotional signals to influence user behavior without the user's conscious knowledge. Creating experiences that support business goals, including persuading consumers to buy a product, give their data, or take a particular action, is frequently the aim.

Appealing to emotions in order to subtly influence decision-making is known as "emotional nudging." For instance, to appeal to customers' fear of missing out (FOMO), an online shopping platform may employ scarcity (e.g., "Only 3 left in stock!") to generate a sense of urgency. Similar to this, social media sites frequently take advantage of users' curiosity or need for social validation by sending emotionally charged notifications to entice them to keep using them.

Although these techniques are frequently successful in raising sales or engagement, they can also have unfavorable effects, especially if they are applied to susceptible groups like adolescents or those with addiction problems.

The Thin Line That Separates Exploitation from Empathy

It's getting harder to draw the thin line between developing empathetic systems and exploitation. On the one hand, emotionally intelligent AI systems can assist users by providing emotional connection, understanding, and support. A social robot created to help individuals with mental health concerns, for instance, might offer comfort and reassurance through therapeutic responses based on emotional analysis.

However, this same technology might be used to exploit emotions for financial gain, influencing people to make choices they otherwise wouldn't, including self-disclosure, excessive spending, or compulsive behavior.

The question of when emotional support becomes emotional exploitation emerges as these systems get more complex. Developers and organizations bear the burden of balancing these issues by making sure that emotional AI systems are designed with ethics in mind.

6.4 Developing Emotional and Ethical AI Systems

Developers must be proactive in creating ethical emotional AI systems in order to reduce the hazards of algorithmic bias, privacy violation, and emotional manipulation. Adoption of ethical frameworks, adherence to guidelines, and cooperation among ethicists, developers, and policymakers are necessary for this.

Responsible Development: Principles, Frameworks, and Guidelines

The following should be part of an ethical emotional AI framework:

- Transparency: Developers are required to give users explicit notice regarding the collection, usage, and storage of emotional data. The consequences of interacting with AI systems that monitor emotional reactions should be completely understood by users.

- Fairness: Algorithms need to be made as impartial as possible. To avoid prejudiced results, this involves making sure that emotional AI systems are trained on diverse data sets that represent different demographic groups (e.g., race, gender, age).

- Accountability: Organizations and developers are accountable for the moral application of emotional AI systems. This entails keeping an eye out for negative consequences and being ready to make changes when systems inadvertently cause harm.

The Function of Ethicists, Developers, and Policymakers

- Policymakers: Governments ought to enact laws that protect users' emotional privacy and guarantee the responsible use of emotional AI. This could entail establishing data protection laws that are unique to emotional data and imposing restrictions on its usage.

- It is the duty of developers to incorporate ethical standards into the AI design process. This involves making certain that privacy safeguards are incorporated into the system and that biases are mitigated during the training process.

By spotting possible moral conundrums and offering frameworks for responsible design, ethicists are essential in directing the development of emotional AI. They can assist legislators and engineers in navigating the difficult moral terrain of emotional AI.

The ethical issues raised by emotional AI have been examined in this chapter, ranging from algorithmic bias and the risks of emotional manipulation to privacy concerns. It is evident that emotional AI carries a number of serious concerns even if it has the ability to completely transform human-machine interactions. Therefore, to guarantee that new technologies advance society without endangering it, a cautious and ethical approach to their development and implementation is necessary.

CHAPTER 7

TECHNIQUES FOR MULTIMODAL EMOTION RECOGNITION AND FUSION

Over the past ten years, emotion detection systems have seen tremendous change, progressing from single-modality analysis to more intricate multimodal techniques. Multimodal emotion identification aims to enhance the system's capacity to precisely detect and interpret emotions by using the capabilities of integrating several data sources, including visual, aural, and textual cues. This chapter explores the several methods for multimodal emotion recognition, the difficulties that arise, and the possibility of incorporating these systems into practical uses.

7.1 Combining Textual, Visual, and Auditory Cues

In order to produce a more comprehensive and precise understanding of human emotions, multimodal emotion recognition attempts to combine several sensory modalities, including text, speech patterns, and facial expressions. These systems are better able to overcome the inherent constraints of each specific modality by utilizing multiple types of data.

Improving Precision With Multimodal Evaluation

A more thorough examination of an individual's emotions is made possible by the distinct and complementary insights that each modality visual, aural, and textual offers into emotional states.

- Visual cues: People frequently believe that a person's facial expressions are the best way to gauge their emotional state. Specific facial movements (such as smiling, frowning, and raised eyebrows) that are associated with emotions like happiness, grief, or surprise are analyzed using Facial Action Units (AU). However, in certain situations, such as when people conceal their feelings or use deceptive facial expressions, visual cues alone may be misunderstood.

- Auditory cues: Tone, pitch, rhythm, and speed all convey a great deal of emotional information in speech. For instance, faster speech and higher pitch might convey excitement, whereas slower, monotonous speech can convey boredom or melancholy. Another useful audio clue for identifying emotional strain or worry is voice stress analysis. However, when emotions are presented softly or in noisy surroundings, speech-based emotion identification may be difficult.

- Textual cues: Textual analysis, which is frequently carried out through the use of Natural Language Processing (NLP) tools, concentrates on the words and syntax that people use. Words that convey emotion directly include "happy," "excited," and "disappointed." On the other hand, deeper sentiment analysis, which examines the underlying sentiment of a message, may be necessary for more complex emotions. Despite its advantages, textual analysis may not be able to fully grasp context or identify nuanced emotions.

Multimodal emotion recognition systems can get beyond the drawbacks of each cue type by mixing different modalities. For instance, a person's speech or writing may convey more subliminal clues about their feelings than their visual mask. Similarly, when facial expressions are hard to read, text and audio can offer additional context.

Sensor Data Fusion Challenges

Although combining several data sources appears to be a viable approach, sensor data fusion presents a number of technical challenges:

Data Alignment: Coordinating data from several modalities is one of the main obstacles. For example, visual and auditory cues may not precisely coincide in time and are frequently gathered at distinct sampling rates. Misinterpretations of the emotional state may result from this imbalance. To solve this problem, sophisticated synchronization methods are needed.

- It might be challenging to extract significant features from many modalities and combine them in a way that catches all of the pertinent emotional information. To prevent one modality from overwhelming the others, each modality needs its own preprocessing stages, such as speech segmentation and face identification, and the final features need to be properly weighted.

- Computational Complexity: Compared to unimodal systems, multimodal emotion recognition systems require higher computing power. Both hardware and software are heavily burdened by the requirement to analyze massive volumes of data from various sources in real-time.

- Data Imbalance: imbalanced data might result from different modalities providing different amounts of information for each emotional state. Speech data, for instance, may be better at collecting emotions like surprise or embarrassment but may be less good at capturing emotions like anger or excitement. To guarantee that all modalities contribute fairly, this imbalance needs to be carefully balanced during the fusion process.

7.2 Affective Fusion via Deep Learning

Multimodal emotion recognition has evolved significantly thanks to deep learning techniques. The multimodal data streams are typically processed and fused using Convolutional Neural Networks (CNNs), Recurrent Neural Networks (RNNs), transformers, and attention mechanisms.

Attention Mechanisms, CNNs, RNNs, and Transformers

- Convolutional Neural Networks (CNNs): CNNs are very helpful for processing visual data, including video frames or face images. From raw image data, these networks can automatically learn hierarchical properties, including identifying emotion-specific facial expressions. Because CNNs can extract spatial information (such the movement of facial muscles) that correlate with particular emotions, they are widely utilized for emotion identification from facial expressions.

- Recurrent Neural Networks (RNNs): RNNs are perfect for processing sequential data where the order of information is important, like text or audio. RNNs may learn temporal dependencies when used on text or speech, which helps them comprehend how emotions evolve over time. To identify changes in emotional state, RNNs, for instance, can monitor tone or sentiment changes during a discussion.

- The processing of textual data has been completely transformed by the introduction of transformer architectures, especially those utilized in NLP jobs. Transformers, as opposed to RNNs, employ a self-attention mechanism that enables the model to assess each word's relative importance inside a phrase. Because of this, transformers are quite good at managing distant dependencies and comprehending intricate, contextual linguistic interactions.

The model may concentrate on the most pertinent aspects of the input data at any given moment with the use of attention processes. Depending on the emotional situation, attention mechanisms can be used in multimodal fusion to prioritize particular modalities. For example, the model might prioritize speech signals above facial expressions in a noisy setting, or vice versa.

Transfer Learning for Tasks With High Emotional Content

Transfer learning is the process of fine-tuning a model on a smaller, emotion-specific dataset after it has been pre-trained on a large dataset for a general task. In multimodal emotion recognition, this method has demonstrated considerable potential, particularly in situations when data scarcity is an issue.

- To increase accuracy in emotional recognition tasks, pre-trained models, such BERT for text analysis or VGGNet for picture recognition, can be adjusted. This method has the advantage of lowering the quantity of data needed for efficient emotion recognition by allowing the models to use previously learnt features that might be applicable to other domains.

- Multimodal transfer learning: Multimodal systems can also benefit from transfer learning. For instance, audio and text data can be added to a model trained on visual emotion recognition as a starting point for multimodal systems. This makes it possible to quickly create reliable emotion identification systems without having to gather a lot of data from every modality.

7.3 Temporal Emotion Tracking and Synchronization

The capacity of multimodal emotion detection to monitor emotions throughout time is one of its main advantages. The operation of temporal emotion tracking and the significance of real-time synchronization of emotional updates are the main topics of this section.

Instantaneous Emotional Updates and Impact Pathways

Emotional changes continuously must be tracked in many

applications, particularly those involving human-computer interaction or mental health monitoring. Systems can modify their reactions in response to changes in emotional states thanks to real-time emotion updates.

- The emotional paths that people take over time are referred to as "effect trajectories" and can provide information about how emotions change and interact. For instance, a person may become neutral at the beginning of a conversation but become frustrated, angry, and calm throughout the exchange. By monitoring these trajectories, models are able to predict future emotional states in addition to detecting the emotion at the moment.

- In situations like mental health monitoring, where identifying changes in mood might predict emotional crises or initiate interventions, real-time tracking is essential. For example, monitoring a patient's emotional development during a treatment session may assist medical professionals in determining whether a patient is becoming more stressed or anxious.

Recognizing Changes in Emotion Over Time

- Emotional dynamics can be better understood with multimodal emotion identification systems that can track emotions throughout time. Understanding the complexity of how emotions evolve and impact behavior is more important than simply identifying an emotion at a particular moment in time.

- A number of things, including contextual changes and external stimuli, can cause emotional shifts. It is necessary to comprehend both the emotional state at any given time and the context in which those feelings arise in order to comprehend these changes. For example, if someone displays anger After hearing terrible news, it might be a temporary emotional response, but persistent annoyance could indicate deeper problems.

- Systems can respond more effectively to emotional dynamics by modifying their responses in accordance with temporal emotion tracking. To maintain a pleasant interaction, a customer service chatbot could, for instance, recognize a change from frustration to satisfaction and modify its responses accordingly.

7.4 Datasets and Benchmarking

The creation of efficient emotion identification algorithms is mostly dependent on evaluation metrics and high-quality datasets. Some of the most popular emotion recognition datasets are described in this section along with how emotion recognition models are benchmarked using them.

Overview of Datasets for Emotion Recognition

- AffectNet: With over 1 million facial photos annotated with various emotional states, AffectNet is one of the biggest and most varied databases for facial emotion identification. Deep learning algorithms for visual cue-based emotion recognition are frequently trained using this dataset.

- Audio, visual, and text data are all included in the

Interactive Emotional Dyadic Motion Capture (IEMOCAP) dataset, which is a multimodal dataset. It is perfect for training and testing multimodal emotion identification systems because it comprises recorded emotional discussions.

- Anger, happiness, melancholy, and frustration are among the emotions for which IEMOCAP contains labeled data.

Assessment Measures and Generalization Across Datasets

Utilizing evaluation metrics that can gauge accuracy across various datasets and modalities is crucial for assessing emotion recognition systems. Typical evaluation metrics consist of:

- Accuracy: Indicates the proportion of emotions that are accurately identified.
- When working with unbalanced datasets, the F1-Score provides a beneficial balance between precision and recall.

- A key component of real-world deployment is cross-dataset generalization, which guarantees that a model trained on one dataset performs well on unknown datasets.

Multimodal emotion recognition is an area that is developing quickly and has a lot of promise. Technical challenges including computing load, fusion complexity, and data synchronization still exist, though. The future of emotion recognition appears bright thanks to the ongoing development of deep learning methods and the accessibility of bigger, more varied datasets.

CHAPTER 8

SOCIAL AND CULTURAL ASPECTS TO TAKE INTO ACCOUNT

Cross-cultural and social concerns are crucial for developing emotion recognition systems. Despite appearing to be universal, emotion detection differs greatly among cultures, languages, and social contexts. Developing systems that are both efficient and considerate of the variety of human experiences requires an understanding of the complex ways in which emotions are expressed, understood, and reacted to. This chapter examines how social norms affect how emotions are displayed and perceived, how language affects emotional semantics, and how cultural differences affect emotional expression.

8.1 Cross-Cultural Expression of Emotion

Although emotional expression is frequently assumed to be a universal human experience, cultural differences in how emotions are expressed can be significant. Many emotions are strongly impacted by cultural norms and values, even though some may be generally acknowledged.

Emotion Markers: Universal vs. Culture-Specific

According to Paul Ekman and other emotion researchers, there are a number of basic emotions that are universally conveyed through facial expressions, including happiness, sorrow, anger, surprise, contempt, and fear. It is thought that these feelings have developed to convey crucial survival information. Although there may be biological bases for the manifestation of these fundamental emotions, cultural settings can influence how they are expressed, understood, and controlled.

- Facial expressions: While some cultures hide or mask emotions like grief or rage with more neutral facial expressions, others openly display them. For example, although East Asian cultures, which are influenced by Confucian ideas, tend to emphasize emotional restraint and social harmony, Western cultures may encourage people to express their feelings more freely.

- Body language and gestures are also influenced by cultural variations. For instance, expansive hand gestures frequently accompany emotional emotions in Latin American cultures, but Nordic cultures may place more emphasis on preserving personal space and reducing expressive gestures.

- Vocal tone: Although tone and pitch are important for expressing emotions in many cultures, there are differences in how these vocal cues are interpreted. A raised voice, for instance, may be interpreted as angry in certain cultures but as excitement or enthusiasm in others.

The existence of universal emotional expressions is supported by data, but in order to prevent misunderstandings, emotion-aware systems must take into account local variations in emotional cues.

Emotion-Aware System Localization

Localizing emotion recognition models is essential to creating emotionally intelligent systems that work well in various cultural situations. Beyond merely translating words, localization takes into account the larger cultural context in which feelings are felt and communicated.

- Emotion recognition systems must be trained on datasets that reflect the cultural diversity of their target users. This is known as cultural sensitivity in data collecting. When implemented in non-Western environments, a system that was trained on Western-centric datasets might not function well. Datasets must be reflective of a broad spectrum of body language, emotional standards, and cultural emotions in order to lessen this.

- Cultural diversity model adaptation Machine learning models should be built to identify cultural markers in emotional expression, such as group-specific gestures, expressions, and linguistic patterns. In many cultures, for example, smiling may signify happiness, but in some communities, it may also represent politeness or nervousness. To guarantee that emotional interpretation is culturally appropriate, these minute variations must be incorporated into the model.

- The effectiveness of emotion identification in global applications can be increased by localizing emotion-aware systems, which allows developers to produce tools that are more accurate and considerate of a variety of demographics.

8.2 Emotional Semantics, Language, and Dialects

Language is essential to emotional expression because it influences how people express their feelings and understand those of others. The development of emotion identification systems is made more difficult by the fact that different languages and dialects have unique methods of expressing emotions.

Comprehending Contextual and Idiomatic Expressions of Emotion

There are many idiomatic expressions in languages that

have deep emotional meanings that a literal translation might not always convey. Accurate emotion recognition requires an understanding of these idioms.

- Idiomatic phrases: Expressions such as "feeling blue" or "on cloud nine" in English we communicate feelings of despair or happiness, respectively, but translating each word alone is insufficient to understand them. For instance, "avoir le cafard" (literally, "to have the cockroach") indicates that one is down or depressed in French. To effectively detect emotions in textual data, emotion identification algorithms need to be able to recognize certain types of idiomatic expressions.

- Contextual language: Depending on the situation, words and phrases might have several meanings. Depending on how it is used, a single word in various languages can convey a variety of feelings. For example, depending on the situation, the English term "love" might denote intense adoration, familial ties, or romantic attachment. To correctly interpret emotional meaning, emotion-aware systems must be able to recognize contextual clues, such as surrounding words, tone, and sentence structure.

Cross-Linguistic Emotion Detection with AI Language Models

The usage of AI language models, such BERT or GPT, to identify emotions in text is growing. To comprehend the nuances of emotional expression in different languages, these models must be taught.

- Emotion detection algorithms trained on English text may have trouble detecting emotions in languages with distinct syntactic patterns or cultural backgrounds. For instance, emotions may be conveyed subtly through verbs or sentence endings in Chinese or Japanese rather than explicitly through adjectives (as in English). Therefore, in order to effectively assess emotional tone across languages, emotion detection systems need to be customized to particular linguistic elements.

- The development of multilingual models has made it

possible to identify emotions in a variety of languages without the requirement for distinct models for each language. Although linguistic diversity must be present in the training data to guarantee cross-language robustness, these models are capable of learning cross-linguistic patterns in emotional expression.

- International applications will yield more accurate results when emotion-aware systems that take into account the richness of linguistic variation are better able to comprehend emotions as they are presented in many languages.

8.3 Emotion Display Guidelines and Social Norms

How people express and perceive their emotions is governed by social norms and cultural expectations. The appropriateness of expressing emotions in particular contexts is determined by display rules that exist in many cultures.

Emotional Communication and Cultural Expectations

People are expected to control their emotional emotions in various social contexts in order to conform to social norms. Depending on the group's expectations, emotions may be suppressed, amplified, or distorted as a result of these display guidelines.

- Collectivistic vs. individualistic cultures: Individualistic cultures, like those seen in many Western nations, place a strong focus on self-expression and the manifestation of one's own feelings. Conversely, collectivistic cultures, like those seen in many East Asian nations, place a strong emphasis on social harmony and may urge people to repress or conceal feelings that would jeopardize group cohesiveness.

- Power distance: People may be expected to hide or downplay their emotions in front of authoritative people in societies with high power distance. On the other hand, regardless of one's place in the hierarchy, emotional displays may be more openly expressed in low power distance societies.

- Public vs. private settings: While some cultures prefer more stoic behavior in public, others may permit emotional expressions in private. This is especially true in formal settings when emotional outbursts are deemed improper or unethical, such business meetings or social events.

Modifying Reactions Using Social Etiquette

Systems that are sensitive to emotions need to be able to identify the social setting in which they are being expressed. For instance, depending on whether the user is speaking in an informal or formal context, the system might need to modify its emotional response. Systems used in customer service applications need to be able to distinguish between situations in which a customer's frustration is a casual, less important emotion and those in which it is based in a social context that calls for a careful, courteous response.

In certain cultures, people are trained how to control their emotions in public. Emotion detection systems in these situations should refrain from overinterpreting small emotional indicators, which may not always reflect the person's actual feelings but rather the cultural expectation to keep emotional control.

8.4 Developing Emotional AI with Global Sensitivity

The development of emotion-aware systems that are cognizant of cultural differences around the world is crucial as AI is further incorporated into systems intended to communicate with a variety of demographics. This calls for the creation of inclusive and culturally aware AI that considers the entire range of emotional expression and experience.

Developing Culturally Aware Training Models and Inclusive Datasets

An emotion detection system needs to be trained on inclusive datasets that cover a broad spectrum of emotional circumstances and cultural expressions in order to be genuinely effective on a global scale. Diverse data from individuals of various ethnicities, ages, genders, and social backgrounds must be gathered for this purpose.

- Inclusive data collection: To avoid bias, datasets used to train emotion recognition models must include a variety of cultural groups. This will guarantee that the algorithm can correctly identify the emotions that people from different backgrounds display.

- Training models must also adjust to the local emotional display norms. This is known as cultural adaptations in training. For instance, AI systems ought to be more perceptive to subtle emotional clues than overt facial expressions in societies where people may conceal their feelings.

Collaborating with International Partners

The development of culturally sensitive and inclusive emotional AI requires developers to co-create with stakeholders from many backgrounds and cultures. This strategy aids in making sure the system respects and is pertinent to the users' cultural background.

- Working together with cultural specialists: To comprehend the emotional expression conventions in various cultures and locales, developers ought to collaborate with specialists in anthropology and cultural studies. These professionals can offer insightful information about the complexities of feeling that could be missed otherwise.

- Continuous feedback from global users can assist improve emotion recognition algorithms and guarantee that they continue to be accurate and culturally responsive in a variety of settings.

The development of tools that function well in a globalized world requires the creation of emotionally intelligent systems that are cognizant of cultural and social factors. Developers may produce accurate and courteous systems that promote stronger ties between people and technology by taking into account cultural variations in emotional expression, comprehending the significance of language and social norms, and building internationally responsive AI.

CHAPTER 9

FUTURE DIRECTIONS AND EMERGING FRONTIERS

Thanks to study, technological improvements, and a better understanding of human emotions, the subject of emotion artificial intelligence is growing quickly. New frontiers are opening up as we look to the future, especially in fields like brain-computer interfaces (BCIs), the metaverse, and artificial creatures with synthetic emotions. With an emphasis on these ground-breaking technologies and the interdisciplinary partnerships required to influence their advancement, this chapter examines the potential future paths of emotion AI.

9.1 The Metaverse and Emotion AI

Emotion AI has the potential to significantly improve virtual and augmented reality (VR/AR) environments as the world grows more and more engrossed in them. A collective virtual shared space called the metaverse has the capacity to produce emotionally engaging experiences that mimic or even outperform interactions in the real world. Making these virtual environments emotionally compelling and socially significant will require the use of emotion AI.

Sensing Emotions in VR/AR Settings

Sensing and interpreting emotions will be essential for producing genuinely realistic VR and AR settings. In contrast to traditional media, which passively expresses emotions through sound and images, VR and AR allow consumers to engage with their surroundings in real time. A range of sensory inputs can be used by emotion AI to identify emotional reactions, including:

- Facial expressions: VR and AR systems are able to track a user's facial expressions using sophisticated computer vision techniques, identifying small emotional alterations in real-time. The virtual world or characters can then be modified using this data to produce more interesting and customized experiences.

- Voice modulation: A user's tone, pitch, and pace can all give away a lot about how they're feeling. These vocal signals can be evaluated by emotion AI in conjunction with speech recognition software to ascertain a user's emotional state in the virtual environment.

- Posture and body movement: In virtual reality, people communicate by making gestures and moving their bodies. These movements can be recorded by wearable technology or sensors, which allows the system to identify emotions from physical reactions such as posture, tension, or even minute changes in movement speed.

In order to improve immersion, these emotional cues might be employed to construct dynamic environments that react to the user's emotional state. In a virtual reality game, for example, a player's growing anxiety may result in more intense or sinister situations, whilst a more relaxed condition may result in more tranquil interactions.

Building Virtual Environments That Inspire Emotions

Beyond merely detecting emotions, the incorporation of Emotion AI into the metaverse has the potential to create emotionally intelligent virtual environments. Based on the user's emotional input, these places will change and develop to provide a highly individualized virtual experience. Among the potential uses are:

- Emotion-driven narrative experiences: Systems that are sensitive to user emotions can change a virtual world's plot according to the user's feelings. The setting may heighten the game's horror features if the user is afraid, whereas a happy user may encounter more upbeat and cheerful virtual environments.

- Adaptive avatars: Avatars can be made to respond to a user's emotional state in a variety of ways, either by reflecting their feelings or by acting in ways that encourage tranquility or interaction. For example, if a user is frustrated, their avatar may show empathy by making gestures or facial expressions that imply comprehension.

- Customized interactions with other users: Users can engage in real-time interactions with other avatars in the metaverse. Avatar interactions can be analyzed by emotion AI, allowing for more responsive and sympathetic exchanges. By guaranteeing that emotional subtleties are acknowledged and respected, this could improve social interactions and online communities.

Our interaction with digital worlds could be revolutionized by the ability to perceive and react to emotions in virtual environments, making them more emotionally compelling and immersive.

9.2 Brain-Computer Interfaces (BCIs) with an affective component

One of the most promising and ambitious areas of emotion artificial intelligence in the future is brain-computer interfaces, or BCIs. Bypassing conventional input techniques like keyboards or touchscreens, these technologies establish a direct communication channel between the brain and external equipment. It is anticipated that as BCIs advance, they will be able to directly decipher emotions from neural impulses, providing previously unheard-of control and insight into human emotional states.

Direct Emotion Decoding Using Neural Signals

Real-time brain activity interpretation by BCIs may make it possible to directly decode emotional emotions. Brainwave patterns or variations in blood flow linked to emotional reactions can be measured using methods such as electroencephalography (EEG) and functional magnetic resonance imaging (fMRI). As these technologies advance, they might be capable of:

- Identify emotional states in real-time: BCIs may be able to identify an individual's emotional states such as happiness, sadness, anxiety, or stress by examining brain signals, even if the individual does not express them directly.

- Monitor emotional shifts: BCIs may also be able to identify minor changes in emotions over time, providing information about how emotions change in response to certain stimuli or during daily life.

- Allow for direct involvement with emotional states: Through neurofeedback, BCIs may eventually give users control over their emotional states. By directly altering brain pathways, BCI-based technologies, for instance, could help people control their anxiety, improve their mood, or even improve their cognitive function.

Application in Cognitive Enhancement and Neurofeedback

Additionally, the fields of neurofeedback and cognitive enhancement could be transformed by affective BCIs. These technologies may help users better understand and regulate their emotions by giving them real-time feedback on their emotional and cognitive states.

- Stress reduction: By using a BCI, people can track how they react emotionally to stress and learn how to control their emotions, which enhances mental health and overall wellbeing.

- Cognitive training: By assisting people in managing emotional states that could impair focus or concentration, BCIs may be able to improve cognitive function. A BCI might, for instance, be able to recognize when a user is getting frustrated or distracted and encourage them to practice relaxation techniques in order to get back to a more focused state.

Better mental health, improved performance, and more direct communication with the brain's emotional processes are all made possible by the use of BCIs for emotional control.

9.3 Artificial Beings' Synthetic Emotions

The idea of artificial beings that display emotional behaviors has been a topic of philosophical, ethical, and technical discussion as AI develops further. Is it OK for machines to have emotions? If so, how can we tell the difference between real-life experience and emotional simulations?

Do Machines Need to Feel? Technical and Philosophical Implications

There are philosophical and technical arguments for and against AI having emotional intelligence. The nature of emotions and consciousness are at the center of the philosophical controversy. Do emotions need sensory experience or are they just preprogrammed reactions? Should we aim to design computers with some kind of emotional consciousness, or should we build machines that mimic emotions to make them more relatable?

- Emotional simulation: The majority of AI systems in use today mimic emotional reactions using datasets and algorithms, but they do not feel emotions in the same way that humans do. Although these simulations facilitate more natural interactions between AI and humans, they do not suggest any kind of consciousness or self-awareness.

- Authentic experience: According to some

academics, an AI that is capable of feeling emotions would necessitate a degree of consciousness and self-awareness that is currently unattainable in machine development. The difficulty lies in determining whether simulation is adequate for functional engagement or whether genuine emotional experience is required for AI to possess emotional intelligence.

Real Experience vs. Emotional Simulations

Emotional simulations can be useful even if AI is not able to sense emotions like humans do. Emotion-aware AI can improve human-to-human interactions by simulating emotions using algorithms that replicate human emotional responses, including empathy or sympathy.

- Empathy in AI: Although AI cannot "feel" empathy, it can be taught to react to human emotions in an empathetic manner. Applications such as robotic caregiving, where robots are made to comfort or help humans without requiring emotional participation, may benefit from this.

- Emotional manipulation: However, the capacity to replicate emotions presents moral questions. Is it possible for artificial intelligence to negatively impact human emotions, such as by using them to promote goods or sway public opinion? It's important to carefully examine the boundaries between emotional manipulation and real emotional engagement.

In addition to raising important ethical and philosophical issues regarding the nature of consciousness, agency, and emotional integrity in artificial creatures, the development of synthetic emotions in AI has the potential to improve human-machine interactions.

9.4 Future Multidisciplinary Partnerships

As Emotion AI develops further, it becomes evident that interdisciplinary collaborations will be essential to the technology's future. For Emotion AI to be developed in a responsible and efficient manner, psychology, ethics, AI, design, and policy must all be integrated.

Integrating Psychology, Ethics, AI, Design, and Policy

Emotion AI systems will be able to comprehend and react to human emotions in ways that are consistent with human behavior and thought processes thanks to insights from psychology.

- The responsible development of Emotion AI will be heavily influenced by ethical considerations, especially with regard to privacy, consent, and emotional manipulation.

- AI and Design: AI developers and designers will collaborate to build systems that are emotionally intelligent in addition to being functionally effective, making sure that emotional reactions are meaningful and appropriate for the context.

- Policy: To guarantee that Emotion AI is created and implemented in ways that put human welfare, autonomy, and privacy first, policymakers must establish rules and regulations.

Developing the Upcoming Emotionally Intelligent System Generation

These several sectors will work closely together to develop the next generation of emotion AI. Experts can guarantee that Emotion AI is not only technically sophisticated but also morally upright, emotionally intelligent, and socially conscious by cooperating. This will entail developing systems that value human emotions, improve communication between humans and machines, and advance societal well-being in general.

Emotion AI has a bright future ahead of it, full with revolutionary possibilities. The possibilities are both thrilling and difficult, ranging from emotionally charged virtual environments to brain-computer interfaces (BCIs) that can decipher neural feelings. However, interdisciplinary cooperation, ethical considerations, and a thorough comprehension of both human emotions and computer capabilities will be necessary for the creation of these systems. As Emotion AI develops further, it will surely influence how we use technology and reshape the limits of human-machine interaction.

CHAPTER 10

CREATING A RESPONSIBLE EMOTIONAL AI ECOSYSTEM

There has never been a greater need for ethical and responsible design methods as artificial intelligence (AI) advances. The ability of emotional AI to recognize and react to human emotions makes it a potent tool with enormous potential to enhance social interactions, user experience, and even mental health. But there are also new moral and societal obligations that come with using emotion AI. Establishing an ecosystem that minimizes dangers like bias, manipulation, and breach of privacy while guaranteeing that these technologies benefit society as a whole is essential. This chapter examines the development of a responsible emotional AI ecosystem through co-design techniques, industry standards, education, and legislation.

10.1 Emotional AI literacy and education

Education is the first step towards building a responsible emotional AI ecosystem. Both users and developers must have a thorough awareness of the technology's potential and constraints in order to promote a society in which Emotion AI is applied morally and successfully. To make sure that everyone can use this technology responsibly and make educated decisions, it is imperative to develop emotional AI literacy.

Providing Knowledge to Users and Developers

- Knowing the technology: It is essential to educate developers, businesses, and the general public on how emotional AI functions. People must understand that AI systems are not able to "feel" emotions in the same way that people do. Instead, they mimic empathy or emotional reactions by analyzing and reacting to patterns in human behavior, such as body language, voice tone, and facial expressions.

- The intricacy of emotion detection systems and the possible repercussions of creating systems that profoundly engage with human emotions must be understood by developers in particular. This information will assist in preventing unforeseen outcomes, such as the use of AI to influence decisions or emotions.

- Emotional literacy: The capacity to recognize, comprehend, and appropriately express emotions is another necessary skill for users of Emotion AI systems. With this knowledge, people may use these technologies in productive and healthful ways. For instance, users must be able to decipher AI-driven information about their emotional states in therapy or counseling apps that use emotion detection.

AI Literacy and Emotional Awareness Education in Schools

It is recommended that all educational levels incorporate emotional AI literacy into their courses. Students must comprehend both the technological and human components of emotional intelligence as they grow up in a society that is becoming more and more reliant on technology. Students can learn about AI's operation, ethical ramifications, and how to preserve emotional health in the digital age in school.

- Building critical thinking abilities: Students should be trained to evaluate the ethical implications of AI critically, especially when it comes to its affective components. They ought to comprehend not just the architecture of these systems but also the ways in which they interact to influence interpersonal relationships and human behavior.

- Building emotional intelligence in the classroom: By including emotional intelligence instruction into the curriculum, students can gain social skills, empathy, and self-awareness that will enhance their understanding of how AI interprets emotions. Students who possess emotional literacy will be better able to interact with AI technology in a meaningful manner and comprehend both the possible advantages and disadvantages of these systems.

The impact of emotional AI on society will grow as it gets

more pervasive. Therefore, a crucial first step toward a responsible emotional AI ecosystem is making sure that everyone, from developers to consumers, has the resources and know-how to interact with these technologies appropriately.

10.2 Frameworks for Regulation and Policy

Emotion AI and other AI technologies are being adopted at a rapid pace, necessitating the creation of extensive legal frameworks to direct their research, application, and deployment. To guarantee that these tools are used in a way that is moral, open, and respectful of human rights, policymakers, business executives, and technologists must work together to create guidelines and standards.

National AI Strategies and International Guidelines

- worldwide cooperation: Since AI is a global phenomenon, it is critical to develop worldwide standards that build a common strategy for emotional AI. Areas like privacy, security, accountability, and transparency in AI systems should all be covered by these rules. To guarantee that moral behavior is maintained globally, institutions such as the United Nations and the European Union might be crucial in establishing these international norms.

- International norms are vital, but each country must also create its own AI strategy that takes into account its own legal, cultural, and economic circumstances. To make sure the technology doesn't take advantage of people's emotional weaknesses, violate their privacy, or reinforce prejudices, governments can enact legislation requiring emotional AI developers to follow specific ethical standards.

- AI ethics in policy: National AI strategies need to incorporate ethical principles. These guidelines ought to guarantee that AI developers give fairness and transparency top priority when creating systems that handle emotions. Guidelines may, for instance, require AI systems to notify users when they are processing sensitive information and give them authority over the use of their data.

Establishing Accountable and Open AI Governance

- Transparency: AI systems must function openly, particularly when handling sensitive data like emotions. Users ought to be able to access details on the collection, processing, and storage of their emotional data. Additionally, the decision-making process in these systems ought to be transparent. For instance, the user should be notified of the data inputs that resulted in the conclusions drawn by an emotion-recognition AI if it offers insights on the user's emotional state.

- Accountability: Companies and developers need to answer for the things their AI systems do. This entails establishing distinct lines of accountability in cases when the emotional reactions of an AI system are applied in ways that are detrimental to people or society. For instance, a corporation should be held accountable and the proper sanctions should be in place if an AI program unethically manipulates emotions to boost user engagement.

- Auditability: Consistent audits of Emotion AI systems can assist in guaranteeing adherence to accepted ethical standards. These audits should evaluate AI systems' privacy, fairness, and transparency policies to make sure that the sensitive data they process is handled carefully.

Governments and organizations can guarantee that emotional AI is implemented responsibly and ethically, protecting user rights while optimizing the technology's potential advantages, by establishing efficient regulatory and policy frameworks.

10.3 Best Practices and Industry Standards

Fostering uniformity, accountability, and trust throughout the AI ecosystem requires the establishment of industry standards and best practices for the creation and application of Emotion AI. These guidelines ought to specify what ethical emotional AI is as well as the procedures and tools that ought to be applied to guarantee the security, equity, and dependability of these systems.

Creating Certification Organizations and Benchmarks

- Benchmarks: Industry benchmarks offer a way to gauge how well emotional AI systems perform and adhere to ethical standards. These standards might include things like the capacity to manage bias, the transparency of data processing, and the accuracy of emotion detection. By establishing these standards, developers and users will have a clear understanding of what makes an AI system responsible.

- In order to confirm that emotional AI systems adhere to accepted ethical norms, independent third-party certification bodies can be quite helpful. By certifying AI developers, these organizations may reassure the public that their creations have undergone testing for emotional accuracy, equity, and adherence to privacy laws.

Promoting Community-Driven Standards and Self-Regulation

Establishing a culture of self-regulation within the AI community can support the upholding of ethical standards and promote innovation, even while external rules are crucial. In order to build and improve community-driven standards that can be adjusted to the changing environment of emotional AI, AI developers and businesses should actively collaborate.

- Collaborative frameworks: Developers can collaborate to develop frameworks that tackle issues like algorithmic bias, transparency, and data privacy. The AI community may freely exchange these frameworks to encourage best practices and prevent effort duplication.

- Ethical AI innovation: It is crucial to promote a dedication to ethical innovation. There should be incentives for developers to produce ethically sound and emotionally intelligent AI. Building a responsible emotional AI ecosystem can be facilitated by the AI industry by emphasizing privacy, fairness, and transparency throughout the development process.

10.4 Developing Emotionally Ethical AI Together

Developing AI systems with emotional ethics calls for a cooperative and inclusive strategy. It is essential to include the people who will engage with these systems in the design process rather than creating AI in a vacuum. We can guarantee that emotional AI systems are not only highly advanced technologically but also in line with human values and ethical standards by using a human-centric approach to development.

Including Users in Affective System Development

- User feedback: Incorporating people into Emotion AI's design and testing phases might yield priceless insights into how these systems affect actual experiences. Developers can learn from users how emotional AI systems should react in various situations and how to be open and honest about their workings.

- Inclusive design: AI systems should be created with inclusivity in mind, taking into account the various cultural settings and emotional demands of various user groups. For instance, because emotions are exhibited and understood differently in different cultures, an AI that recognizes emotions may function differently for people from different backgrounds.

Cooperative Development and Human-Centric Innovation

- Designing with empathy: Developers need to make sure that their designs show empathy and take users' emotional health into account. This entails creating systems that are both sensitive to the possible psychological effects of engaging with AI and capable of appropriately interpreting emotions.

- A more balanced and comprehensive approach to the creation of Emotion AI will be achieved by involving a range of stakeholders, including ethicists, psychologists, AI developers, and consumers. We may create systems that are more in line with moral standards and human values by accepting different points of view.

Creating a responsible emotional AI ecosystem requires a multifaceted strategy that incorporates industry standards, education, regulation, and collaborative design. Fostering a culture of accountability, openness, and moral decision-making is crucial as emotional AI develops to make sure that these potent technologies advance mankind without endangering it.

ABOUT THE AUTHOR

 Author and thought leader in the IT field Taylor Royce is well known. He has a two-decade career and is an expert at tech trend analysis and forecasting, which enables a wide audience to understand complicated concepts.

Royce's considerable involvement in the IT industry stemmed from his passion with technology, which he developed during his computer science studies. He has extensive knowledge of the industry because of his experience in both software development and strategic consulting.

Known for his research and lucidity, he has written multiple best-selling books and contributed to esteemed tech periodicals. Translations of Royce's books throughout the world demonstrate his impact.

Royce is a well-known authority on emerging technologies and their effects on society, frequently requested as a speaker at international conferences and as a guest on tech podcasts. He promotes the development of ethical technology, emphasizing problems like data privacy and the digital divide.

In addition, with a focus on sustainable industry growth, Royce mentors upcoming tech experts and supports IT education projects. Taylor Royce is well known for his ability to combine analytical thinking with technical know-how. He sees a time when technology will ethically benefit humanity.

www.ingramcontent.com/pod-product-compliance
Lightning Source LLC
LaVergne TN
LVHW051653050326
832903LV00032B/3790

* 9 7 9 8 3 1 6 9 8 1 8 8 5 *